Snowbound

Snowbound

Poems for Winter Days

S T Kimbrough, Jr.

foreword by J. Richard Watson

RESOURCE *Publications* · Eugene, Oregon

SNOWBOUND
Poems for Winter Days

Copyright © 2020 S T Kimbrough, Jr. All rights reserved. Except for brief quotations in critical publications or reviews, no part of this book may be reproduced in any manner without prior written permission from the publisher. Write: Permissions, Wipf and Stock Publishers, 199 W. 8th Ave., Suite 3, Eugene, OR 97401.

Resource Publications
An Imprint of Wipf and Stock Publishers
199 W. 8th Ave., Suite 3
Eugene, OR 97401

www.wipfandstock.com

PAPERBACK ISBN: 978-1-7252-5475-6
HARDCOVER ISBN: 978-1-7252-5476-3
EBOOK ISBN: 978-1-7252-5477-0

Manufactured in the U.S.A. 01/08/20

Contents

Foreword by J. Richard Watson	vii
Introduction	xi

1. Snow, Snow, Snow

1. Below Zero Degrees	2
2. Cold Winter	3
3. "Ole Man Winter"	4
4. Ole Man Winter's Pest	5
5. More Snow I	6
6. More Snow II	7
7. Snow Is Simply Snow	8
8. Snow Time	9
9. Snowdrift / Snow Storm	10
10. No Snow?	11

2. Snow Moods

11. A Blanket of Snow	14
12. Shovel Snow and Sing	15
13. A Change of Face	16
14. A Walk in the Snow	17
15. Snowy Moods	18
16. Snow Again!	19

3. The Danger of Snow

17. To Slip on Ice	22
18. Take Care	23
19. An Aborted Walk in Snow	24
20. Shoveling Snow	25

21. Snowfall	26
22. Hello Again!	27

4. The Charm of Snow

23. Sparkles of Snow	30
24. Mother Nature's Charm	31
25. Mother Nature's Dance	32
26. Weather Chess	33
27. Wind and Snow	34
28. A Flake of Snow	35
29. Uncharted Territory	36
30. Snow Casts a Spell	37
31. Silken Scarves of Snow	38

5. The Joy of Snow

32. Sun, Snow, and Fun	40
33. A Snowflake's Brevity	41
34. A Postcard Snowman	42
35. Snow at Last	43
36. Snow-capped Peaks	44
37. A Bird on Snow	45
38. A Close-by Meal	46
39. Nature Joy	47
40. Montana Blizzards	48
41. November Snow	49
42. Kisses from Heaven	50
Appendix	51

Foreword

S T Kimbrough, Jr., is a graduate of the Divinity School of Duke University, and holds a Doctorate in Old Testament and Semitic Languages from Princeton Theological Seminary where he also taught Old Testament studies. For many years he was Associate General Secretary for Mission Evangelism of the General Board of Global Ministries of The United Methodist Church. As an author and editor, he is an internationally known expert on the work of Charles Wesley, and on early European Methodist history in general. He is also a most distinguished singer, and a fine musician.

Now in his eighties, he might be thought to have deserved a rest from his labors. But in 2018 he gallantly answered a call from a United Methodist Bishop in Northern Europe to assist with congregations in Lithuania. He was there from shortly after Epiphany until Easter, through the coldest and most unpleasant time of the year, "just the wrong time of the year for a journey, and such a long journey," as Lancelot Andrewes put it in the sermon that T. S. Eliot used for the beginning of "The Journey of the Magi."

I knew that Steven Kimbrough (his stage name as an opera singer), or "S T" (his legal name), as he is universally known as an author, wrote poetry. His poems written on the death of his beloved wife Sarah, entitled *Of Death and Grief*, were published by Wipf and Stock Publishers in January 2018. They were sub-titled "Poems for Healing and Renewal," and that was an accurate description: They were poems by someone who was, like the figure in Psalm 84, passing through the vale of Baca and made of it a well. The present poems show the same courage, the same ability to make art out of difficult times. They vividly record his time in Lithuania. He calls them "Snowbound," after the title of his wife's painting "Snowbound Trees" that appears on this book's cover. He was, however, literally, bound in by the snow. It fell, day after day, restricting the things that he could do, confining him to a room that looked over a parking lot, limiting his daily exercise to stumbling and dangerous walks over cobbled streets and icy roads. It was a kind of imprisonment, relieved only by the perception that it could not go on forever, though at times it obviously felt that it might. Even then, however, there were glimpses here and there of hope, times when the sun sparkled on the ice to give a magic moment amid the drab greyness of the Lithuanian morning.

View from the author's hotel room. The amount of snow that had fallen during the night can be seen on the railing on the room's balcony.

Foreword

Yet, between gray mornings and falling snow, S T had the courage and energy to write poems about this experience. He did so, writing poems in which the snow becomes a reflection of his changing moods. In "Shovel Snow and Sing" he has an upbeat moment, celebrating seasonal change; but the next poem, "A Change of Face," returns to the dirt and slush of winter. He walks out, careful not to fall, treading in the footsteps of others like the page in "Good King Wenceslaus," bumping his head on a tree branch, watching birds fighting for a scrap of something edible. He finds himself wondering at snowflakes in their beauty and brevity, and he appreciates, too, the sparkle of sun on the rooftops, the moonlight on the cobbled streets, and the quiet that falls when the snow has kept most people indoors.

Undaunted by his experience, he returned to Kaunas in 2019, answering the call to go back to Lithuania and assist the congregations there. He became quite ill during this second visit and at one point he had difficulty in taking services in the local churches. In addition, he had a very bad fall, in which he damaged his right hand and arm. A few poems from this second trip are also featured in this collection. Together with those from 2018, they form the record of a unique experience. They are written in a conventional poetic style, which will delight many readers, and which occasionally provides in the rhymes, moments of surprise and delight. I commend them to all those who like traditional poetry, and who wish to participate, even at second hand, in something of a remarkable experience.

J. RICHARD WATSON
EMERITUS PROFESSOR OF ENGLISH, UNIVERSITY OF DURHAM, UK.

Introduction

IN THE TOWNS AND cities of northern Alabama, where we had lived in my childhood and youth, there were occasional winter snows. And, during the Second World War, when my father was stationed as a chaplain at the Army Air Corps base in Lincoln, Nebraska, our family had its first encounters with the severe plains, winter storms of middle America. There it was so cold that on some afternoons after school my sister, Mimi, and I could go ice skating on a lake not far from our house.

The author, the little boy on the right, is pictured with his sister and maternal grandmother, Estelle Starr Butterley, just after a heavy snowfall in northern Alabama.

Introduction

In the winter of 2018, however, I was destined for a new snow experience. I arrived in Kaunas, Lithuania, in January of 2018. I had been there many times before, even at the height of winter when snow blanketed the ground. My first trip to this charming Baltic nation was in November 1994. At that time, as a staff member of the General Board of Global Ministries of The United Methodist Church I was charged, in the wake of the demise of Communism, with the search for remnants of The Methodist Church, which had begun in Lithuania at the turn of the last century, ca. 1900, through the outreach of its predecessor the Methodist Episcopal Church.

Much to my delight, not only did I discover the charming old Methodist Church building in the city of Kaunas, but I met three members of the Owaldas family, two sisters and a brother (Antonina, Liongina, and Honoratus), who were in attendance at the last worship service in June of 1944, when the Communists closed the doors of the Kaunas Methodist Church for the last time and confiscated the land and building.

Within a year after my arrival, the process was under way to reclaim the Kaunas Methodist property and in August of 1995 the Kaunas congregation was reconstituted and held its first worship service under the leadership of Bishop Hans Växby.

Now I had returned twenty-four years later at the invitation of the United Methodist bishop of Northern Europe and Eurasia, Christian Alsted. This time, however, the purpose of my journey was quite different. I had been asked to serve as an interim clergy to two congregations in the towns of Kybartai and Pilviškiai. The plan was for me to serve them for a little over two months through the celebration of Easter. This little book is part of the story of my sojourn.

Growing up in Alabama and Nebraska, I had experienced winter snow, but never had I known what it was like for six or seven weeks to see snow on the ground every morning with the temperature never rising above the freezing mark.

Now I was in Lithuania where people are accustomed to severe winters. I was staying in the city of Kaunas, the second largest city of the country. Vilnius, the capital city, was about an hour and a half's drive away.

There was snow on the ground when I arrived, and every morning the first thing I would do was to look out of my hotel window to see whether more snow had fallen during the night and whether it was coming down at that moment. Though it often had snowed during the night, still more flakes might fall the next morning. Just a block away from my hotel was the

INTRODUCTION

Neman River, which rarely freezes in winter because of its steady currents. However, during my stay, much of the river was frozen. One morning I recall seeing a gentleman riding his bicycle along the river on the ice.

As we drove through the countryside, time after time I saw numerous frozen lakes and ponds spotted with ice fishermen, hoping to catch their lunch or dinner through the openings they had made in the ice, so that they could reach the water beneath with their fishing lines.

The fields were blanketed with beautiful white snow, and here and there I saw empty stork nests, nestling atop electrical wire poles, that had been abandoned for the winter and now were topped with little pillows of snow, a charming sight.

A snow-covered street in Kaunas, Lithuania.

Every morning I could not resist writing about the snow which has such a multi-faceted charm. Each afternoon I would take half-mile walks through the old city of Kaunas, whose architecture and cobbled streets

Introduction

decked in snow held a special fascination all their own. Some days upon returning to my room I would record the experiences of my walks, encounters with a bird, the cobblestones, the wind, the snow, the people. The result is this little book of snow poems.

While I could make no claim of understanding the depth and heart of an Alaskan or a Yukon winter, I experienced in Lithuania for the first time what it was like for endless weeks to awaken to snow in the morning and see it outside my window every night before retiring.

I do recall a winter trip in the 1990s to Russian Siberia, namely, to the city of Vladivostok, in the month of January. There was no snow but the wind-chill factor was minus ten degrees centigrade and the wind off the bay was so strong one evening that I thought I would not reach the front door to my hotel, which rested on a hill above the bay. I had to lean forward into the wind and push with all my strength just to get to the hotel. I can imagine what it might be like there in a driving snowstorm.

In another part of Russia, namely Kaliningrad-Oblast, which before World War II was Germany's East Prussia, I was once in the main city Kaliningrad at the height of a January winter. This was not long after the demise of Communism, and the city had little infrastructure. As a result, the heavily fallen snow remained in the streets so long that automobiles, busses, and trucks had left deep ruts perhaps more than a foot deep. This soon made the streets impassable so the traveling vehicles took over the sidewalks which became the main thoroughfares of the city. Such a sight I had never seen before.

One of my first Sundays turned out to be a very special occasion in the town of Kybartai. This small town lies adjacent to the border between Lithuania and the only part of Russia that is separated from the land mass of Russia proper. It is known today as Kaliningrad-Oblast. It was formerly East Prussia and the city known today as Kaliningrad was once the German city of Königsberg. After World War II, Russia was permitted to retain this wedge of territory between Poland and Lithuania.

On February 9, 1909, the first Methodist church building on Russian soil, for Lithuania was then part of Imperial Russia, was dedicated by Bishop William Burt. One hundred and nine years later, it was my special privilege to be present on the anniversary of this significant day, which I celebrated with the following poem.

Introduction

Kybartai 1909/2018

We celebrate the saints of yore,
    who gave their lives for us unknown.
Their story is for us not lore,
    but evidence of love they've shown.

'Twas in a little border town,
    Kybartai was the place by name,
they built a church; would not back down
    their faith as Methodists to claim.

A country claimed then by the Tsar
    of Russia's vast imperial realm,
the Wesleyan roots were sown afar
    with Christ their Savior at the helm.

The year was nineteen hundred nine,
    ten decades plus nine years ago.
New saints have risen as a sign
    faith did not die, rather did grow.

A respite of some fifty years
    with Communists, the reigning power,
this faithful band were without fears,
    to suffering they did not cower.

The church, the building, was torn down,
    a thoughtless act of those who dared
to try to stamp out faith and drown
    the saints; and many were not spared.

Today in their small building's space,
    the Methodists again do pray
and sing with joy of God's rich grace.
    They tell you: We are here to stay.

                Feb. 9, 2018

Introduction

My Lithuanian snow experience was much gentler than my January-Siberian venture, as my poems reflect, but it was an experience of diverse beauty that I shall never forget. I was completely enchanted by the wonder of creation in this part of the world.

In 2019, I returned to Lithuania during the winter for almost three months again with similar responsibilities. Much to my surprise there was almost no snow at all. Hence, the only resulting poem was "A Snowflake's Brevity" (#33). Two poems were inspired by a 2019-trip to Bozeman, Montana and Yellowstone National Park in the USA, namely, "Snow-capped Peaks" (#36) and "Montana Blizzards" (#40). "A Postcard Snowman" (#34) was recently written in a humorous mood.

1. Snow, Snow, Snow

1. Below Zero Degrees

The temp has dipped so low again,
    below zero degrees.
The nights are but a painful skein
    of devastating freeze.

The snow has lain upon the ground
    for three or four long weeks.
The wind won't stop its howling sound
    or reddening my cheeks.

I wonder if there will be spring
    or frozen we will stay,
and "Ole Man Winter" will he bring
    more snow and clouds of gray?

Until spring comes in a slow crawl
    to soften the hard ground,
with mother's crocheted, woolen shawl
    my feet I'll wrap around.

2. Cold Winter

Cold winter is a torturous test
    for those disliking snow.
It certainly provides no rest,
    no matter where you go.

You trudge along, your boots half full
    of snow that's cold, and yet,
the snow's so deep your socks of wool
    are soggy and all wet.

The snow abruptly turns to sleet,
    and then it turns to rain.
You're drenched all through! Yes, it's complete!
    Cold winter is a pain!

3. "Ole Man Winter"

"Ole Man Winter" just won't let go.
    Is he still here for spite?
He keeps on raining snow on snow
    with temperatures that bite!

For one month now there's no relief;
    my boots I can't keep dry.
Does he not know he causes grief?
    He's certainly not shy!

If he's a man of moods, why not
    change moods one time this year?
Should he be kind, then spring is wrought
    with Ole Man Winter's cheer.

4. Ole Man Winter's Pest

Thirty-five days of snow on snow,
    today it's thirty-six.
The temperature has been so low
    we've had no springtime fix.

Now, "Ole Man Winter," as a force
    can hold back days of spring,
because he's thinking, "Well, of course,
    I'm weather kingdom's king!"

Depending where on earth one lives,
    he rules for months on end.
Siberia scarce relief he gives;
    his will is tough to bend.

But "Ole Man Sol" gives him no rest
    with beams of warming light.
He's Ole Man Winter's natural pest
    till snow is out of sight.

5. More Snow I

The snow has stayed a week or so,
for temperatures have been so low.
I wonder if we'll get a break,
or will we see more flake on flake.

More flakes of snow, "O No!" I said,
"I've swept and swept, can't get ahead.
The walkway to my door is filled;
I shoveled it, but was too chilled,

"Too chilled to finish it, I'll wait,
but rays of sun may be too late;
too late to melt this giant mound,
and I will simply be home bound."

Home bound is not the worst of things,
a better pace for life it brings.
There's time to sit, to read, to think,
to make hot chocolate, what a drink!

So, Mother Nature, bring your snow;
I need nowhere to be or go.
I'll make a fire, sit down and warm,
and let the snow just storm and storm.

6. More Snow II

Snowfall I thought we'd left behind,
    but, no, it's here again.
I thought the weather would be kind
    and snowfall would restrain.

Shall I let seasons change my mood,
    spring, winter, summer, fall?
One season will not make me brood!
    The truth—I like them all.

For weather, there's no second guess.
    It's what it is. That's that!
You don't know if it will bring stress,
    or if you'll need your hat.

So, laugh a bit! Yes, you should laugh,
    for weather's laughing too.
If not, I'll laugh on your behalf:
    snow, rain, storms are for you!

7. Snow Is Simply Snow

Outside my window snow on snow
    blows swiftly here and there.
Up, down, around, where will it go?
    It does not seem to care.

It cares not if on steps it lands
    and makes them slick as glass,
or piled upon the pavement stands,
    so not a soul can pass.

Snow, snow is simply snow, that's all
    that I have left to say,
and I can't wait till spring or fall
    will bring a warmer day.

8. Snow Time

Persistent snow falls yet again,
and winter's long enduring chain
of daily snow, just never breaks,
another day of giant flakes.

Yesterday the flakes were small;
today they're falling in a squall.
Low clouds and bursts of driving snow,
when it will stop, I do not know.

The weather comes, the weather goes,
but why must there always be snows?
Must there be snow as late as March
on Paris's Triumphal Arch?

Or snow that falls in the late spring
in Rome, in Cairo, or Beijing?
My queries are alas for naught,
for I in snow time have been caught.

9. Snowdrift / Snow Storm

The snowdrift rises hour by hour;
    the wind shifts back and forth.
With each new foot of snow its power
    gets stronger from the north.

When will this storm come to an end,
    the wind's sharp howling cease?
And does this storm danger portend,
    a blizzard's chance increase?

I do not know the weather's trend;
    this secret no one knows.
How can one know when storms will end
    and what will stop the snows?

Sometimes a snow storm does surprise
    when no one did expect
that snow would fall, and prove a wise
    prediction was not checked.

So I'll sit by a crackling fire
    and watch sparks rise and fall.
And if the snowdrift gets much higher,
    I'll face a six foot wall.

10. No Snow?

Today, how odd there's no snowfall.
    Has winter truly made a pause,
or has the snow just gone AWOL,
    and left the weather without cause?

No cause? Oh, weather has a cause!
    We just don't know what it will be,
for it's designed by nature's laws
    with pleasant times or misery.

Thank goodness "respite" is a word,
    we hope, that weather seems to know
or it would truly be absurd
    to claim: today there'll be no snow.

2. Snow Moods

11. A Blanket of Snow

What a blanket of snow
    did its magic last night:
twinkling whiteness aglow
    from the moon's glistening light.

It was quiet, no sound
    could be heard 'cross the street.
and as I looked around,
    not a soul did I meet.

For a moment, I stood
    without moving a bone;
never thought that I could
    bask in being alone.

But snow, it is magic,
    for it transports the mind
from all that is tragic,
    till to beauty confined.

12. Shovel Snow and Sing

I hear the sound of shovels scrape
    the pavement at the last snowfall,
by workers who cannot escape
    the task which moves at a slow crawl.

Will rain replace the winter snow
    and bring the advent of the spring,
when flowers bloom again and grow,
    and once again our spirits sing?

If I am honest, I'll admit
    that every season has its songs:
some sad, some happy, some with wit—
    and that is where my heart belongs.

In all the seasons of the year
    I need to learn their songs to sing,
both melancholy and of cheer,
    that every change of mood can bring.

Then every coming season's change
    can touch the heart strings of us all:
discover moods that we'll exchange
    for what fits winter, spring, and fall.

So, shovel snow and sing a song
    for spring is coming, sun and rain,
the autumn colors won't be long,
    and then the snow will come again.

13. A Change of Face

The snow today makes a grim face,
    for boot tracks now turned brown
have left here, there an ugly trace,
    as if the snow would frown.

Would frown because its snow-white sheen
    has vanished with the sun.
The landscape that had looked so clean
    was quickly overrun.

Was overrun by dirt and slush
    so, when you walk along
the ice and snow have turned to mush.
    Has spring done something wrong?

Just then as if the snow would smile
    and stop its angry frown,
it seemed to say with wintry guile,
    "More snow is coming down!"

14. A Walk in the Snow

I walk with snow beneath my feet;
it crunches slowly with a beat,
the beat my steps articulate
with rhythm from my steady gait.

I must be careful not to slip,
the cobble stones oft have a dip,
and should my toe stick in a crack,
I might end up upon my back.

But happily, I go along,
and maybe even sing a song,
or whistle once a jolly tune;
I hope I'll stay to falls immune.

15. Snowy Moods

Tomorrow what will morning bring?
    Will I find snow still there?
If not, I'll hope that spring takes wing
    and weather will be fair.

I must admit I'm weather bound
    so far as changes go;
I'm cheerful or oft brooding found
    when sleet has turned to snow.

For now, I'd better pause and think:
    The weather I can't change!
I'll keep this fact with thoughts in sync,
    lest moods of mine seem strange.

16. Snow Again!

Just a few days the warming trend
    made the illusion plain:
the thaw has come, and spring will send
    its fresh, delightful rain.

But while I slept, I did not know
    what in the night transpired.
I woke, looked out, and saw more snow.
    It's not what I desired.

I thought, "Cheer up, the snow is light.
    It won't stay on the ground."
But—morning, afternoon, and night
    the snow has stayed around!

3. The Danger of Snow

17. To Slip on Ice

The snow was crusty, frozen hard
    as I walked slowly on;
I knew I must be on my guard
    or balance could be gone.

To slip on ice, that is no fun!
    It's dangerous and a dare,
a dare that once around you've spun,
    you're flying in the air.

I do not wish to fall on ice,
    I'll make my steps secure.
Last week I fell, not once but twice;
    for falling there's this cure:

You take your steps: one, two, and three,
    walk in another's track,
for there's the best chance, there's the key,
    you won't land on your back.

18. Take Care

While walking down a cobbled street
    when snow has decked the stones
with pearl-white dust beneath your feet,
    they look like sugar scones.

You move one foot, take one more step,
    then stop before you skid,
like workers of Amenhotep,
    who climbed a pyramid.

19. An Aborted Walk in Snow

Walked out the door again today
    and surely, it was no surprise
that snow had fallen on the way.
    I wondered if the walk were wise.

I could not see the cobblestones;
    car tires had left the faintest tread.
A pine-tree branch decked with snow cones
    I did not see and bumped my head.

The snow cones flew into the air,
    blown higher by the gusts of wind;
the dust of snow then filled my hair,
    as I watched my wool cap descend.

The wind had thrust it to the ground;
    to pick it up, I then bent down,
and as a blackbird flew around,
    it shook more snow upon my crown.

My head was then completely wet;
    I'd only walked a block or two.
I thought, I will this walk forget
    and rethink what today I'll do.

20. Shoveling Snow

My hotel window hovers o'er
    a giant parking lot,
and there a chap has quite a chore.
    Yes, what a job he's got!

The lot is covered thick with snow,
    some cars seem stuck for sure.
His shoveling stops, he looks with woe,
    and knows there's no quick cure.

He cannot wave a magic wand
    and all the snow is gone.
He feels the sweat this work has spawned,
    but he must carry on.

Just then a co-worker appears
    with shoveling tools in hand.
His friend with kindest words then cheers;
    the work by two is manned.

Within an hour the work is done
    and they stand by, shake hands.
Where snow had lain there now was none;
    the pavement now clean stands.

When someone asks the question, Why
    two better are than one?
These fellows quickly testify:
    In just one hour 'twas done!

21. Snowfall

First gently fell some flakes of snow,
    so large I counted one, two, three.
The wind began to howl and blow
    so fiercely one could scarcely see.

So sudden was the wintry blast,
    with blizzard winds and snow in sheets
that counting snowflakes did not last,
    and soon I could not see the streets.

One solitary soul passed by
    as through my window I, by chance,
did catch a glimpse and see her try
    to take a step, a fragile dance.

The wind was fierce and held her back,
    though weak and weary she then turned,
as sailboats on their courses tack,
    came to my house, her snow-trek spurned.

She made it to my door, then knocked;
    I opened, wind and snow rushed through.
"I'm weary and the road is blocked,
    I'm oh so cold! My hands are blue!"

"Do come in quickly," I declared,
    "I have a fire where you may warm."
She stood before it and just stared,
    then whispered: "Oh, I'm free from harm."

22. Hello Again!

The snow just will not let me go;
    I thought I left it here last year.
It greets me now to let me know
    it need not make my mood so drear.

It's just as white as I recall
    those six long weeks without a pause,
when I had luck never to fall
    in spite of gravity's strict laws.

I'll sit a moment to reflect
    on winter's greeting once again.
I wonder, what can I expect?
    Could winter once from snow abstain?

4. The Charm of Snow

23. Sparkles of Snow

Snow sparkles, sparkles in the light
    of moon, daylight, and sun.
If right, the angle of your sight,
    they're playful, on the run.

No single sparkle is the same,
    though you may think it so;
like prisms playing their own game
    the colors, what a show!

As if one turned some kaleidoscopes
    across a vast terrain
and all the earth had brand new hopes:
    and snow's magic could reign.

The magic moments in the snow
    one must be quick to see,
for tragic it would be to know
    you've missed reality.

24. Mother Nature's Charm

The shadows of tree branches dance
    upon the fallen snow;
with beauty they the fields enhance,
    as winds waft to and fro.

It's not a waltz or a fox trot;
    they dance *ad libitum*:
Up, down, around, formal it's not,
    no need of a ballroom.

The dance is nature's way to show
    she never is a bore.
Yes, more than dancing on the snow,
    she has much more in store.

The wind another dance begins
    on housetops, roofs, and trees,
while snowdrifts and the wind like twins
    shimmer beneath the breeze.

Yes, many a tale of joy is born
    from Mother Nature's charm
and some are told from night till morn,
    for fun, not for alarm.

25. Mother Nature's Dance

I saw a gorgeous scene last night,
    the trees were trimmed in snow.
The moon then cast a shimmering light
    on branches, high and low.

The moon painted a silhouette
    upon a field of white,
and dancing branches quickly met
    their partners for the night.

The branches and the light danced on,
    delightful, what a pair!
They danced until the break of dawn
    with Mother Nature's flair.

Then stealthily clouds overcast
    this exquisite, charmed scene,
and dancing could no longer last,
    the moon could not be seen.

Just then the wind took up the dance;
    the trees swayed with delight.
The dance continued, not by chance
    from dawn until the night.

So, Mother Nature's dancing lasts;
    the cycle she repeats!
Enchantment daily o'er us casts—
    her dance o'er fields and streets.

26. Weather Chess

Some snow still lies upon the ground
    awaiting its demise.
Tomorrow will it be around
    with sun and bright blue skies?

Most likely not, that is my guess,
    though I've been wrong before,
and guessing weather is like chess:
    you move, and check's in store.

27. Wind and Snow

It's bitter cold: I'm still outside,
    the wind takes all my breath away.
The howling wind cries out, "Inside!"
    Oh, my! It's there I want to stay.

Alas, alas, so far to go:
    a mile at least and maybe two,
and thicker yet the falling snow;
    and trudge along is all I do.

And then the thought occurs to me:
    the beauty in the wind and snow
surpasses all my agony!
    They're nature's jewels! Don't you know?

28. A Flake of Snow

The wonder of a flake of snow,
    a feathery crystal of ice,
in six-fold symmetry will grow,
    no single flake shaped like a dice.

No two snowflakes alike appear,
    their shapes and patterns so diverse:
hexagonal, never a sphere.
    A different shape one can't coerce.

This gift of nature is unique,
    a tiny flake evokes such awe
that parents cannot wait to peak
    at snowflakes that their children draw.

29. Uncharted Territory

When moonlight falls on frozen snow,
its beams in subtle patterns glow.
Some glitter gracefully, then dance
and hold its viewers in a trance.

Crisscrossing here, there, to and fro,
as if they know not where to go,
uncharted territory theirs,
while some beams seem to dance in pairs.

As moonlight filters through the trees,
the dancing beams dance on with ease.
Their nonchalance a thrill to see
till morning sun makes them all flee.

30. Snow Casts a Spell

The fall of snow can cast a spell
    of visions of a world of white,
where we are privileged to dwell;
    a world that's filled with sheer delight.

I see flakes clinging to the rocks,
    that make up a small garden wall,
and soon the snow's so deep large blocks
    of it will surely, surely fall.

Outside my window there's a tree,
    whose limbs are thickened by the snow;
on one of them a chickadee
    was run off by a cackling crow.

I watched the wind torque left and right
    the snow that lay upon the lawn,
and with a whirlwind to affright,
    it did not cease until the dawn.

By morning light 'twas calm and still;
    the sun caressed the silent snow.
Would that such peace the world could will:
    One morn of peace the world might know.

31. Silken Scarves of Snow

Like silken scarves the snow lay there
    on elevated mountain slopes,
as wind lifts them into the air
    and hums through trees new winter tropes.

What better time to be alive
    than when the sight of nature thrills!
What better time for one to thrive,
    when nature's dancing through the hills!

The painted forest dressed in white,
    the maiden of the wintry dance,
flings back its scarves, O what a sight!
    What wonder do we see by chance!

5. The Joy of Snow

32. Sun, Snow, and Fun

The sun's come out to play today
    upon the fallen snow,
and dancing shadows are at play
    wherever light can't go.

The rooftops gleam as ne'er before,
    and sometimes there's a slide
of snow from roofs that seems to soar
    before it lands beside—

Beside some solitary soul
    who's walking on the street;
out for a daily, pleasant stroll,
    when snow lands at her feet.

She shakes the snow then from her shoes,
    looks up to try to see,
but sunlight blinds her as she rues:
    Is someone after me?

O no, she thought, it's just the sun,
    that shining on a roof,
melted the snow to have some fun,
    and I'm indeed the proof.

33. A Snowflake's Brevity

A snowflake landed on my nose
without a moment of repose.
A moment it was there, then gone,
as other snowflakes carried on.
Each flake has its own form unique.
How fortunate to get a peek.

34. A Postcard Snowman

I thought I'd build a big snowman
    outside in my front yard,
like one I saw from Kazahkstan
    on a large postal card.

He wore a hat like Ghengis Khan
    and had a camel too.
The snow was thick like the Yukon
    or winters in Baku.

I rolled a giant, round snow ball
    till I could push no more,
then took my grandma's woolen shawl,
    which she in winter wore.

A second snowball put on top,
    the shawl then wrapped around,
my cap I knew I'd have to swap,
    Pa's homburg I had found.

It did not look like Ghengis Khan,
    still, best that I could do:
a radish goatee added on
    with snow cream as the glue.

35. Snow at Last

Today the snow has come at last,
    but it's too warm to stay,
and just as in the winters past,
    the wind has had its way.

Some flakes were blown upon the roofs,
    and some clung to the trees
revealing one of winter's proofs:
    spring may not come with ease.

Some flakes on a park bench alight,
    just as the wind dies down,
laid out just like a sheet of white
    or snowwhite evening gown.

They don't last long, a boy comes by,
    scoops up a large snowball;
he packs it, turns; he is not shy;
    throws it at his friend Paul.

36. Snow-capped Peaks

The snow-capped peaks of Yellowstone,
    Great Tetons white peaks too,
seem like a giant ice cream cone,
    on clear days, that's the view.

As if one grains of sugar poured
    across these mountain tops,
or is it sea salt there is stored
    or what a snow cloud drops?

Imagination does run wild
    as one stares at this scene.
Just then a child said, as she smiled,
    "Hey, Mom, that snow looks clean."

Up there, yet, it is wintertime,
    but I've a short-sleeved shirt,
For where I stand it's summertime,
    and wintry peaks avert.

37. A Bird on Snow

A bird did on the snow alight
    as I walked into town.
It pecked the snow without affright,
    though I stopped and looked down.

He pecked and pecked close to my feet;
    I stared with some surprise.
I must admit it was a treat
    to watch him seek a prize.

Just one small piece of grain his beak
    was longing there to find.
My, would it indeed be chic
    to know what's on his mind.

This bird let me stand close to him,
    while he looked for some food.
Most birds would start without a whim
    and fly away for good.

I stood and watched for minutes long
    until beneath the snow
he found a peanut, sang a song,
    and off my friend did go.

38. A Close-by Meal

Last night as snow began to fall
    quite suddenly I heard
outside my window such a squall:
    a sparrow and black bird
were fighting over one last nut,
    that both desired to eat.
The black bird grabbed it with a strut,
    the sparrow in retreat.

I watched the two birds scratch and scratch
    the ground for one more bite;
just one more seed or nut to snatch
    but nothing was in sight.
Now searching for a meal's not hard
    with snow piled inches high;
the hungry birds out in my yard
    find feeders full nearby.

39. Nature Joy

Alas, the last of winter snow
    a ghostly blanket spreads of white,
beneath which springtime pastures grow,
    but briefly they are out of sight.

With dawn of day and beaming sun,
    the blanket white then turns to green,
and with late morning's cattle run
    no longer can the white be seen.

Thus, nature's colors change their hue
    with snow, and sleet, and mist, and rain.
In southern fields are bonnets blue,
    white Queen Anne's Lace upon the plain.

The wonders of geography,
    a soothing, cooling west trade wind,
the secrets of cartography,
    one can't such nature joy rescind.

40. Montana Blizzards

Montana blizzards often freeze
    one's body to the core.
Montana blizzards do not please,
    and no one asks for more.

The quiet of a blizzard morn
    when traffic's at a stop.
Will make you glad that you were born
    upon a high hilltop.

From there you see the blanket white
    that covers far and wide.
The sun comes out, the scene is right
    to take a fresh sleigh ride.

You bring the horses from the barn;
    you hook them to the sleigh,
and off you go, this is no yarn.
    You'll do it every day.

That is, when heavy winds slow down,
    you let the horses start.
And off you go, right through your town;
    the horses, sleigh look smart.

41. November Snow

How can it be—
November first, no snow?
I'm sure I remember
that it fell last year.
I arrived that very day
without an overcoat.
That's why I can't forget.
November first and snow.

The flakes were huge,
falling like giant cotton balls,
clinging to anything still.
They were blinding white
in the sun's unseen rays
and gathered themselves
into a blanket of white velvet.
November first, there was snow!

How can it be
that here again I am,
and early days of winter
bring nothing but the cold?
They disappoint snow lovers,
who love the slower pace
that snowfall always brings.
They await November snow.

Snow lovers know this:
that snowfall brings
more time for love,
more love of nature,
more love of each other.
And they love the quiet
that snowfall always brings.
They await November snow.

42. Kisses from Heaven

Are snowflakes kisses from heaven,
    as is so often said,
each one a unique form given
    when water and cold wed?

The snowflakes on the earth alight
    as if tiptoeing by.
At times in blizzards, what a sight
    as in large sheets they fly!

In snowdrifts snowflakes lose their form,
    as they're together bound,
and at the end of every storm
    no unique forms are found.

Each snowflake lives, each snowflake dies,
    just as we all will do.
Till then, enjoy each kiss heaven tries
    to share with me and you.

Appendix

Additional Photo Images of Snow in Lithuania in the Winter of 2018

People walking in a pedestrian zone filled with snow in Kaunas, Lithuania.

Appendix

Snow-covered grounds surrounding Pilviškiai United Methodist Church in Pilviškiai, Lithuania.

Appendix

Old Town Square in the city of Kaunas, Lithuania.

Appendix

Wooded area outside The United Methodist Church in Kybartai, Lithuania, as seen on a winter Sunday morning.

www.ingramcontent.com/pod-product-compliance
Lightning Source LLC
Chambersburg PA
CBHW071752040426
42446CB00012B/2525